SIDE-SADDLE

by
Jane Pryor

Illustrations by
Carole Vincer

KENILWORTH PRESS

First published in Great Britain by
Kenilworth Press, an imprint of Quiller Publishing Ltd

British Library Cataloguing in Publication Data
A catalogue record for this book is available from the British Library

ISBN 978 1-905693-03-0

Printed in Great Britain by Halstan & Co. Ltd

Disclaimer of Liability
The author and publisher shall have neither liability nor
responsibility to any person or entity with respect to any loss or
damage caused or alleged to be caused directly or indirectly by the
information contained in this book. While the book is as accurate as
the authors can make it, there may be errors, omissions and
inaccuracies.

KENILWORTH PRESS
An imprint of Quiller Publishing Ltd
Wykey House, Wykey, Shrewsbury, SY4 1JA
tel: 01939 261616 fax: 01939 261606
e-mail: info@quillerbooks.com
website: www.kenilworthpress.co.uk

CONTENTS

INTRODUCTION

Riding side-saddle has a long history. It started with lady riders being seated sideways on a horse that had a cushion strapped to it and the horse was usually led. Over centuries improvements for grip, security and independence have brought us to the saddles we ride in today.

The use of the horse for sporting purposes – rather than simply transport – necessitated the saddle being equipped to allow a lady to sit safely but with freedom to carry her hawk or to follow hounds. The pommels (curved leg supports) were introduced – originally two on top of the saddle for the rider's right thigh to sit between. Later this arrangement was improved by the addition of the leaping head (or lower pommel), which the rider needed in order to jump fences and not be sprung off the top of the saddle. The 'third' pommel (the top right-hand one) gradually became smaller and eventually disappeared.

Saddles were very ornate, with fancy stitching and quilting, pockets on the offside flap for gloves and handkerchiefs, and some of the seats were highly decorated with needlepoint. In time all these accessories were dispensed with for reasons of practicality. Ladies who took to the hunting field required working saddles (although one wonders how they managed with their flowing skirts and tight corsets).

The shape of the saddle seat also underwent changes, starting out as a dipped seat and flattening out to become completely flat or with a very slight dip according to the lady's preference. A dipped seat forces the rider to the back of the saddle and is very tiring to ride on; a flatter seat allows the rider to sit in a relaxed and balanced way, enabling her to be more in tune with her horse at all paces.

The majority of side-saddle riders today enjoy upholding the traditions and customs of dress etiquette and the air of style and elegance which goes hand in hand with side-saddle riding.

TYPE OF HORSE OR PONY

There are no set rules for the ideal horse or pony to carry a side-saddle but certain features help, particularly when it comes to fitting a side-saddle.

Most of the saddles we use today were made between 1900 and the 1950s, and it must be borne in mind that in those days horses were a different shape, kept leaner and fitter for hunting and probably did not have the influence of draught or Warmblood breeding giving a heavier shoulder.

The horse should be at least four years old, though it is preferable to wait until he is five and has had time to fully mature and be confident in work. He should have reasonable manners, be willing, forward-going and obedient to the rider's aids.

No special training is required to accustom the horse to a side-saddle.

The horse should be of correct proportions to make a pleasing picture with the size and build of the rider.

A horse that is known to rear up should not be considered for side-saddle under any circumstances.

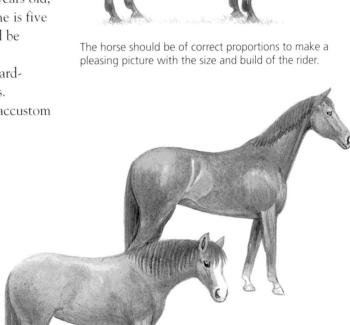

A horse with good conformation will usually be ideal for side-saddle, having reasonably defined withers, a good shoulder and length of rein. A flat-backed animal (above left) with 'no' withers can be extremely difficult to fit and finding a suitable saddle is also a challenge.

TYPES OF SADDLE

PARTS OF THE SADDLE – SHOWN ON AN OWEN SADDLE

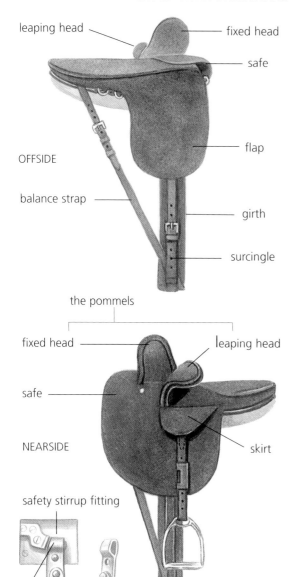

leaping head

fixed head

safe

flap

OFFSIDE

balance strap

girth

surcingle

the pommels

fixed head

leaping head

safe

NEARSIDE

skirt

safety stirrup fitting

A

OWEN saddles are made with a rounded skirt and the stirrup fittings are slightly complex. If the latter do not fit each other perfectly, minor adjustments can be made by careful filing of the inside of the metal loop where it meets the hook at A.

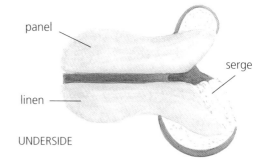

panel

serge

linen

UNDERSIDE

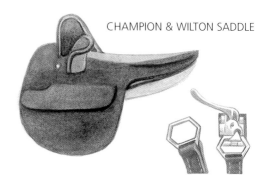

CHAMPION & WILTON SADDLE

CHAMPION & WILTON saddles have a wider skirt on the left side covering the stirrup fitting which ensures that the stirrup leather cannot come off if the rider's right leg is in the correct position.

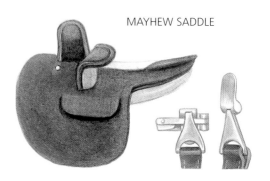

MAYHEW SADDLE

MAYHEW saddles have an oblong-shaped skirt and their stirrup fitting is probably the simplest of the three.

Other well-known makes include Whippy (similar to Mayhew), Robson of York and, in America, Martin & Martin.

Although side-saddles were made by a variety of saddlers there are three makers whose saddles are recognised and favoured worldwide – Owen, Champion & Wilton, and Mayhew. All have distinctive features (the stirrup fitting in particular) and riders often find one maker's saddles suit their needs better than another. Some saddles have doeskin (suede) seats and pommels whilst others are leather seated. Different pommel shapes can be found on all makes, as well as straighter or slightly dipped seats.

The pommels were made to fit the lady for whom the saddle was intended, and can be narrow or wider and flared. The essential factor with the pommels is that the fixed head should be able to accommodate the rider's right thigh; if it is too far to the left the rider will find it hard not to slip to the left and have difficulty sitting square to the front. The former can be remedied with the aid of padding attached to the fixed head. If the pommel is too far to the right, the saddle will be unsuitable as the rider will not be able to position herself correctly.

Most saddles have a partial linen lining which is stitched over the serge on the underside of the panel. The linen 'bearers' as they are called, can be unpicked and rolled back to allow stuffing to be adjusted to ensure the saddle is a good fit.

Panels can be leather lined but these are difficult to adjust without separating the panel from the main part of the saddle.

A Wykeham pad is a panel made of felt. It is an alternative to the usual wool-stuffed panels seen on most saddles. It fits onto a saddle with pockets for the tree points and buckles which match up to straps on the saddle itself. Wykeham pads are an excellent choice for wider horses such as cobs. Wykeham pads can also have a linen lining and a small amount of stuffing to allow fine adjustment to the fitting of individual horses.

As with all saddlery, side-saddles should be cleaned and soaped regularly. Care should be taken not to get soap on any areas of doeskin, which should be kept clean with careful use of a brush. The linen can be wiped with a damp, coarse cloth but care should be taken not to over-wet it.

AMERICAN CLASSES
Extra appointments used in American Ladies' Hunter Classes

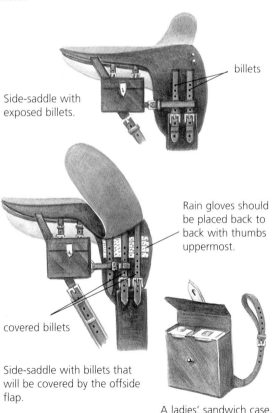

billets

Side-saddle with exposed billets.

Rain gloves should be placed back to back with thumbs uppermost.

covered billets

Side-saddle with billets that will be covered by the offside flap.

A ladies' sandwich case.

FITTING THE SADDLE

One of the most common mistakes in saddle fitting is to place the saddle too far forward, thereby restricting free use of the shoulder. The saddle should be positioned well behind the offside shoulder, with the seat level when viewed from the side. If the tree is too narrow for the horse the saddle will appear to be **sitting uphill.** It is a mistake to pad the rear of the saddle to raise it as the tree points will press onto the horse at the front and not only be very uncomfortable for him but also put undue strain on the tree.

When viewed from behind, the saddle should be slightly higher on the left side to compensate for the rider's weight once in the saddle. There should be no gaps (called 'bridging') and the long point (tree point on left side of saddle) should not dig in on the nearside nor have a gap.

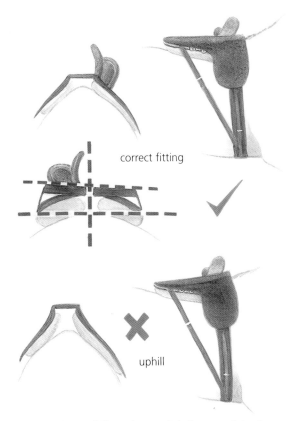

correct fitting

uphill

Saddle coming over to the left: it is often necessary to remedy this by altering the stuffing in the right-hand front rather than more at the left-side back.

Saddle sitting 'uphill': make sure it is far enough back behind the shoulder. If the saddle is too wide for the horse it may ride up the horse's neck, particularly if the balance strap is done up too tightly,

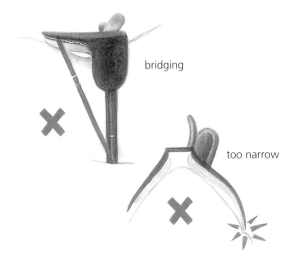

bridging

too narrow

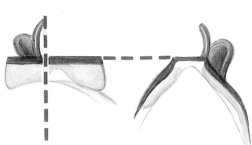

Saddle over to the right: stuffing may be too bulky in the rear of the panels; long point (tree point on left side of saddle) may be too tight in the horse's shoulder.

8

The girth and balance strap should be attached to the nearside (left) of the saddle and all adjustments made on the offside (right). Once the rider is mounted it is very difficult to access the girth straps on the left because her legs cover the flap. Getting the girth as high as possible on the nearside before mounting is recommended. The balance strap should not be done up as tightly as a girth; it is there to help the back of the saddle remain steady but not static. If the balance strap is done up too tightly the saddle will not move with the horse and a rubbed, sore back or scald will occur, possibly making the horse unwilling to accept the side-saddle again. The balance strap is an aid rather than an essential and a well-fitting saddle can be ridden on without one; it should never be relied upon to keep the saddle from slipping to the left.

As a general guide, compare the correct fitting of a saddle to wearing one's own shoes: if too big they are never comfortable, even if thick socks are worn; and no explanation is necessary concerning shoes that are too tight.

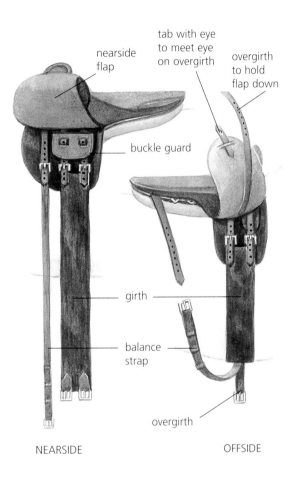

NEARSIDE   OFFSIDE

Saddle too high at the back. Check that the tree is not too wide for the horse, in which case another saddle with a narrower tree should be tried.

excess padding

If the saddle is too narrow it will be perched on the horse rather than fitting round him. In these cases alternative saddles should be sought. It is not satisfactory to put padding in the front of the too-large saddle or to put padding at the back of the too-small saddle to raise the front.

9

TYPES OF GIRTH AND STIRRUPS

The most popular type of girth in use today is the **three-fold leather**, being both hard-wearing and comfortable for most horses. In the folds it should have a piece of fabric which can be soaked in oil to keep the girth soft and supple.

The **Atherstone** girth is popular because of the shaping at the elbows. It is a single piece which is cut and shaped, folded and stitched in the centre on the outside and a plain piece of strap is stitched over the join, the folds being rounded adding to the comfort. It can also have padding in between the folds.

The **Balding** girth originated in the polo field but the design is aimed at avoiding chafing at the elbows. To create the shape, cuts are made in the body of the leather and the resulting straps crossed over to form the almost plaited shape.

Lampwick girths are made of a cotton mixture and are flat and tubular with two buckles stitched at either end. They are undoubtedly the best girths to use on a fat or unfit horse as they are the least likely of all to cause galling. They are usually made in either brown or white and are cleaned by washing.

The **Fitzwilliam** girth is rarely seen these days but is worthy of mention. It consists of a broad, single, flat layer of webbing or leather and has keepers for a thinner girth to be threaded through to lie on top. The advantage being that all three girth straps are utilised. The broader girth is very kind to fat and unfit horses.

Girths with elastic inserts are **not** recommended for use with a side-saddle as they can either be done up too tightly or allow too much give at an inappropriate moment.

Buckle guards should always be used on the nearside to prevent wear into the flap from the girth buckles.

All girths should have either a loop stitched to them at an angle where the girth lies directly under the horse's belly, or the girth should be passed through a loop of leather in order to hold the balance strap and surcingle in place and to prevent them from slipping backwards to create a bucking strap.

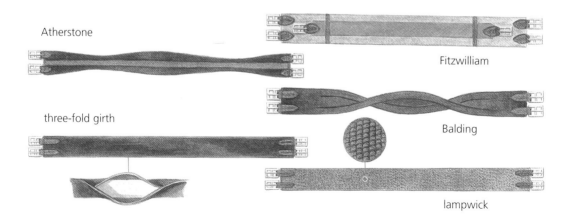

Atherstone

Fitzwilliam

three-fold girth

Balding

lampwick

All girths, regardless of material, must be kept clean and well maintained for safety and to avoid galling the horse.

Stirrup irons

Stirrup irons for side-saddle are designed to assist the quick-release mechanism to function properly in the event of a fall. It is important to ensure that the iron is the correct way round at all times. There's an easy way to remember this: the curved side hangs next to the horse when the leather is hanging straight on the saddle.

The eye of the iron is open and rounded so the leather with its hook can be passed through it. The treads usually have three bars across, the toe end being the rounded one, or the smooth edge to the heel.

Safety irons, which come open to free the foot in an emergency, often have 'HEEL' stamped on them to ensure they are hung on the leather the correct way round. They were designed at a time when saddles had roller bars, a square loop with a roller of leather or metal on the lower part to allow a stirrup leather (of a similar design to astride) to pass through. Although these irons are known as 'safety irons', their use with a roller bar does not provide anywhere near the release properties of the patented stirrup fittings shown on page 6.

If the balance strap is not correctly secured it can slip backwards to become a bucking strap.

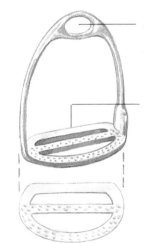

enlarged eye to allow hook fastener on leather to pass through

smooth edge to heel

Side-saddle stirrup iron.

Safety irons with quick-release mechanisms.

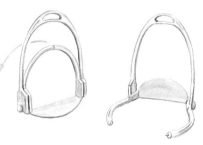

TIP

Never hang a stirrup iron over a pommel. It can tear or damage the pommel's suede or leather. Always remove the leather and iron when leading the horse.

11

MOUNTING AND DISMOUNTING

ASSISTED MOUNTING

1   Standing facing the horse's side, the rider should offer a bent left leg (at or about 90°) so the assistant can place a left hand under the knee and a right hand under the ankle.

2   When springing up, the rider should twist herself so as to land sitting on the saddle facing the left.

In order to mount side-saddle there are several methods that may be employed but initially a leg-up is probably the most suitable. The rider must stand back a little to allow room for herself to get on the saddle behind the pommels, and face the side of the horse as for astride mounting with a leg-up. Novices may find it easier at first to be legged-up astride but can graduate to being put on so as to land in the side-saddle riding position. It is essential to have a person who is capable of legging-up correctly, and it can be helpful to have another person at the horse's head until the procedure is mastered.

MOUNTING FROM THE STIRRUP

Mounting from the ground (or mounting block) using the stirrup. Care should be taken to check that the girths are sufficiently tightened before attempting to mount from the stirrup.

IF WEARING A HABIT

Mounting: place the 'spare' of the apron over your left arm; once you are in the saddle the apron can be placed correctly as shown on page 21.

Dismounting: remove the apron's elastic from the right toe and place the 'spare' of the apron across your left arm. Once dismounted, wrap the apron round your right side and behind you to meet the button on the left-hand side so you do not get tangled in it when walking.

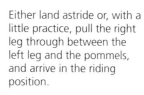

Either land astride or, with a little practice, pull the right leg through between the left leg and the pommels, and arrive in the riding position.

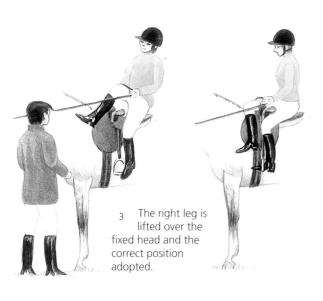

3   The right leg is lifted over the fixed head and the correct position adopted.

ALTERNATIVE METHODS OF MOUNTING

1. Some riders prefer the assistant to stand alongside the horse's shoulder as shown, with knees bent and hands cupped for the rider to step into with the left foot and, on command, both straighten up and the rider lands as in the sequence shown left.

2. Another method employs the same actions from the assistant but the rider continues upwards and places her right leg over the fixed head, arriving in the saddle as she intends to ride. This way is the neatest and worth practising so as to achieve a smooth, polished movement.

DISMOUNTING

1   Take the left foot out of the iron, reins in right hand.

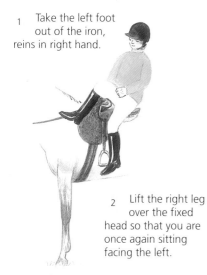

2   Lift the right leg over the fixed head so that you are once again sitting facing the left.

3   An assistant, if you have one, can offer to take your left hand to steady your descent.

4   Slip carefully down to the ground, turning to face the horse as you descend, taking care to avoid catching the pommels on the way down.

5   A bend of the knees as you land (or a little bounce if you have a very tall horse) will prevent jarring injuries occurring as you meet the ground.

ASSISTED DISMOUNTING

It used to be said that one should look round for the most eligible gentleman to assist you when dismounting. However, assisted or not, the procedure is the same.

THE RIDER'S POSITION

Correct position of rider viewed from front and behind.

Holding the balance strap whilst swinging right leg over horse's neck.

Leaning forward to feel weight coming off seat bones.

Correct position for the legs, showing space behind back of right knee and pommel; the left leg has enough space for the hand to fit between pommel and thigh.

The rider should appear to be sitting forwards and straight, just as if astride, when viewed from in front or behind.

When learning the correct position it is helpful for the rider to mount astride, settling into the saddle as far forward as possible but still remaining square to the front, then, before swinging the right leg over the pommel, placing the right hand on the balance strap with the thumb facing forwards. This assists in keeping the right hip back when the right leg goes over the saddle. Once the rider has the right leg in position she should make sure she is far enough forward to allow at least two fingers between the back of the leg and the pommel, and the left hand placed flat should fit easily between the leaping head (lower pommel) and the left thigh.

The weight should not be placed on the seat bones but on the right thigh where it crosses the saddle. The easiest way to feel where the weight should lie is for the rider to lean forwards, as if to put her nose on the horse's mane, and feel how the weight has come off the seat bones and is being taken on the right thigh muscle. By raising the upper body carefully, taking special note not to sit back down on the seat bones, the rider will be sitting upright and in the correct position. If she sits down on her seat bones she will find it hard to achieve the correct posture and the back will be rounded, possibly leading to back pain. She is also likely to push both feet forward, which leads to an unbalanced and very insecure position.

The right leg should hang perpendicular, or slightly back towards the left leg, never in front of the perpendicular line, and the left

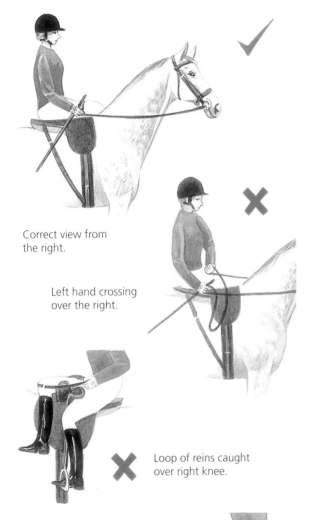

Correct view from
the right.

Left hand crossing
over the right.

Loop of reins caught
over right knee.

leg should be placed so that the stirrup
leather hangs straight down.

For normal riding the left leg should hang
straight down into the stirrup iron. It should
not grip up into the leaping head nor use the
stirrup iron as a lever to achieve gripping up.
The stirrup iron should be regarded as a foot
rest to prevent the leg from getting tired: it
should never be used for weight-bearing or to
stand in, other than when mounting.

The hands should be held in a relaxed
position, with the loop of the reins across the
right thigh, never with the loop over the
right knee, which results in the rein aid only
pulling back on the rider's knee rather than
transmitting to the horse. The elbows should
be sufficiently bent to allow the upper arms
to hang straight down the rider's sides. The
hands should be approximately midway along
the length of the thigh and alongside the
outer right thigh, but discretion should be
used according to whether the horse has a
high, medium or low head carriage. The right
hand should not usually be visible from the
left side and vice versa. It is important to
keep each hand to its own side of the right
thigh, never crossing the right over to the
left side nor the left to the right.

Correct view of hands
and legs from left.

Left leg back and raising
stirrup iron to grip up.
Right toe forward and
downwards rather than
lying in a relaxed position.

Rider sitting too far back,
legs swinging forward.

Gripping up with left
leg, right leg drawn up.

THE RIDER'S AIDS

The aids when riding side-saddle are in essence the same as for astride but with minor differences, notably the cane replacing the right leg. For instance when turning left the rider feels the left rein, applies the left leg on the girth and the cane is pressed on the horse's right side. A firm cane is preferable to a dressage whip, which is too swishy. If the horse does not respond to the pressure of the cane, a small tapping aid can be applied or the cane can be rubbed lightly back and forth to create a sensation via the coat-hair movement. The cane is normally held at 45° with the thumb curled round it, not pointing upwards, which would create stiffness of the hand and arm.

The weight aids differ slightly too in that the rider should not sit down on the seat bones but use the effect created by the turn of the head and shoulders to indicate directional changes to the horse. The right lower leg can also be used to good effect. By pulling it back in order to lighten the right thigh, the horse can be asked for longer strides. By pushing the area just behind the knee down into the saddle and again bringing the right lower leg back, the horse can be asked to slow himself. In both cases the rider must ensure she sits tall and straight rather than allowing herself to collapse in the middle; also her left hip should not slip back. The transition from canter to trot can cause problems: the rider must prepare by making sure the left hip is forward and the right leg is held back. She needs to sit tall and look ahead as the horse moves into the first trot steps, before relaxing into the trot strides. Failure to prepare in this way results in the rider getting thrown about or collapsing in the middle.

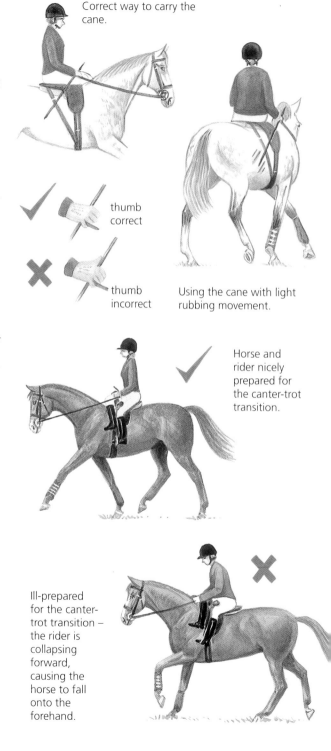

Correct way to carry the cane.

thumb correct

thumb incorrect

Using the cane with light rubbing movement.

Horse and rider nicely prepared for the canter-trot transition.

Ill-prepared for the canter-trot transition – the rider is collapsing forward, causing the horse to fall onto the forehand.

16

JUMPING

Arms too straight on approach.

A good approach with good bend in rider's arms.

Take-off position.

Harmony in flight.

Many riders think they will be unable to jump side-saddle, but with correct beginnings they soon come to enjoy it.

The approach: the rider should retain a contact but with a length of rein whereby the elbows are well bent to allow free giving of the reins during flight. If the approach is made with the arms straight, the rider is likely to be pitched out of the saddle as the horse stretches to rise.

On take-off the rider should move her weight and upper body forwards to go with the horse's movement and allow the hands to move with the contact. The right leg should be well back, and the left leg should remain hanging as straight as possible. There is sometimes a temptation to swing the left leg back – this is a fault and should be corrected as soon as possible as it leads to insecurity on landing. It is equally incorrect to allow the left leg to come forward, again into a very insecure position.

As the horse lands, the rider should ensure that her right hip does not come forward and she should be straightening up for continuing on the flat. It is essential to make sure that

Left leg too far back, right toe gripping up.

Both legs swinging forward.

the left hip is well forward for the point of impact during landing to maintain a strong position. If the right hip gets ahead before landing the rider runs the risk of being spun round to the left and falling off the right side of the saddle.

Some instructors advise shortening the stirrup for jumping but my experience tells me it is unwise to do so as it impedes the left hip from keeping the forward position described above. Unlike riding astride, one length of stirrup leather should suit the side-saddle rider for all gaits and activities.

Start by jumping low fences, and work over small spreads rather than uprights. Spreads makes the horse stretch out whereas uprights produce a somewhat up and down type of jump. Turns to the left should be avoided until the rider is completely confident and secure on landing.

Rider falling off – probable consequence of above faults.

Well-balanced landing with rider giving the horse a comfortable length of rein without loss of contact.

Correct show-jumping position showing rider in a more forward position, ready to take the next jump on landing. This is particularly important when jumping combinations.

The style for **show jumping** differs from cross-country riding in that the whole process is more gathered up and the rider sits in a more forward seat. The reins are held slightly shorter for show jumping, but care should still be taken to have a good bend in the elbows on approach. It is essential for the weight to come right over the right leg, which should be kept back and be the mainstay for the flight. In the case of doubles and trebles, if the rider maintains the above position she will be ready on landing to go straight over the next jump.

Cross-country riding with undulating terrain requires the approach to be more upright, elbows bent, with forward flexion of the upper body when the horse rises and a feeling of going back as the horse begins to land. If the ground is lower on the landing side, the rider must be prepared to meet it and take care to ensure that she keeps her right shoulder back and left hip forward for the stride or two after landing.

The rider has more time between cross-country fences to adjust her position and think ahead to the next fence and its potential difficulties, be it a **ditch in front** (ride more collectedly), a **ditch behind** (ride on more strongly to get over the ditch at the other side), or a **drop** (the most difficult to sit side-saddle as gravity naturally draws the right hip forwards if allowed). **Ditches and banks** are relatively easy as the pommels help you to sit still and allow the horse the freedom to negotiate the obstacle unimpeded.

Riding cross-country at great speed. These riders are in a suitable position to take the variety of obstacles which may be met.

WHAT TO WEAR AND WHEN TO WEAR IT

A well-cut **habit** that fits your figure well will always look smart. The material should be of a good quality and weight, preferably wool, perhaps with the jacket in a slightly lighter weight cloth than the apron, but still of the same weave.

There are a variety of **jacket** styles, some very cut-away, some less so, but a **waistcoat** (or vest) should always be worn, whether complete or as false fronts buttoned or sewn into the jacket. The traditional colour for a waistcoat being a yellowish-biscuit colour similar to the shades used for breeches, although Tattersall check is acceptable. Other colours can be worn according to the occasion – some hunts have particular colours for the waistcoat, and some showing classes allow for other colours. Always check with the governing body's rules or guidelines before entering a competition.

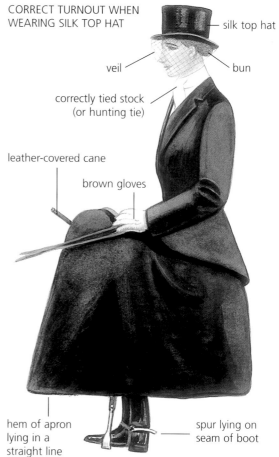

CORRECT TURNOUT WHEN WEARING SILK TOP HAT

- silk top hat
- veil
- bun
- correctly tied stock (or hunting tie)
- leather-covered cane
- brown gloves
- hem of apron lying in a straight line
- spur lying on seam of boot

cut-away   less cut-away

The **apron** should be made of a material which, by way of its own weight, will sit and hang well. It is not a good idea to weight the hem of an apron made of a fabric which is too light with weights designed for curtains and drapes. The hem should be at least 4 inches (100mm) deep and should never be let down; rather add a false waistband to lengthen an apron that is too short. The rider's right foot should be hidden by the apron and the hem, which should run parallel to the ground, approximately 4 inches (100mm) above the rider's left ankle.

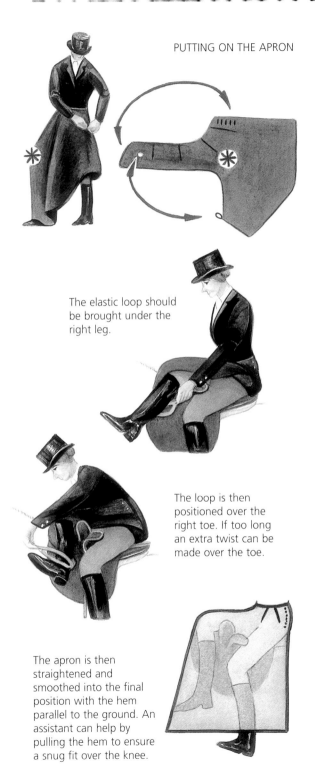

PUTTING ON THE APRON

The elastic loop should be brought under the right leg.

The loop is then positioned over the right toe. If too long an extra twist can be made over the toe.

The apron is then straightened and smoothed into the final position with the hem parallel to the ground. An assistant can help by pulling the hem to ensure a snug fit over the knee.

Habits are usually black, navy, charcoal, brown or tweed in muted tones. Tweed habits are less formal but look smart when used on native or mountain and moorland types. Tweeds are sometimes used for preliminary judging at larger shows, being replaced with the more formal black or navy in the final judging.

A **silk top hat** should be carefully selected to suit the rider's face and height. A lady's hat should be between $4^3/_4$ and $5^1/_4$ inches (120–133mm) tall and worn with the brim parallel to the ground. Hair must be in a bun (false or otherwise) and the hair neatly contained in fine hairnets (it is better to use several very fine nets than one of a heavier gauge mesh). The hair can be dressed either over the ears or behind, according to the rider's preference. The bun should sit directly under the brim of the hat, never down on the collar, and it is a good idea to pin a false bun into the lining of the hat for security. The bun should be about 3 inches (75mm) in diameter and secured with hairpins to prevent it bouncing about, particularly if false. A veil is always worn.

Bowler hats should be of the hardened variety and worn in the same fashion as the silk top hat, complete with veil. Although normally black, brown bowlers can look very smart with certain shades of tweed.

Safety hats with harnesses may be worn and (under most governing bodies) are compulsory for junior riders. Both senior and junior riders would normally be expected to wear safety headwear to current specifications whenever jumping is involved.

Neckwear is dictated by the style of hat being worn. A silk top hat is always worn with a plain white or cream stock (or hunting tie, as it is also known) tied as shown right. It should be secured with a plain pin, which should be worn horizontally (for a lady). The **stock** (or **hunting tie**) can be either of the pre-shaped variety or four-fold, which is probably more preferable. In all cases it should lie flat and not be pulled up and puffed out. The loose ends should be pinned to the shirt to prevent them escaping from within the jacket. When wearing a bowler it is correct to wear a shirt with a snugly fitting collar and a tie. Again, pin the loose ends to the shirt for neatness. The only time a bowler may be worn with a stock is in the hunting field.

Breeches should be of a similar colour to the habit. Leather- or suede-seated breeches can be useful on a leather-seated saddle, which can be shiny and slippery.

Long black **leather boots** are worn either with or without garter straps, and a spur should be worn on the left boot, lying along the seam of the boot, with the strap end well tucked in. If the rider is wearing a brown bowler then brown boots must be worn; it is never correct to mix a brown bowler with black boots and vice-versa. Leather boots should always be highly polished. Rubber boots are acceptable and they too should be polished. Junior riders may wear jodhpur boots.

Gloves should be any shade of brown, ranging from cream through to deep brown. It is never, ever correct to wear black or blue gloves, even if they match your habit.

TYING A STOCK

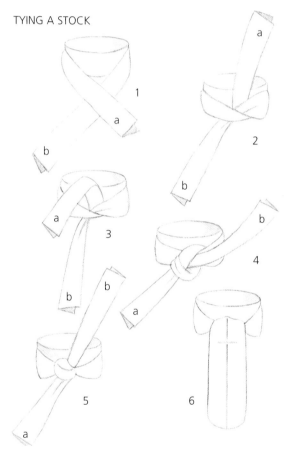

When using a four-fold stock the centre should be placed at the front of the neck and the ends crossed over at the back before tying, as shown.

After tying the knot, as in illustration 5, the fold should be opened out and pinned as in 6.

A shaped stock is tied with the same knot, but on reaching 5, the ends are pulled upwards and outwards before crossing neatly below the knot and securing with pins as for the four-fold.

TIP: If attempting to tie a stock following the above diagrams, it might help you to turn the page upside-down.

Veils should be either black or navy blue (more flattering to the more mature rider) with a black bowler or silk top hat, but if the rider is wearing a brown bowler then a brown veil is used. The veil must be taut with no wrinkles or baggy areas. It is either tied in a small knot at the back of the hat just above the brim, or fixed with elastic tied to each end, which is then crossed over at the back and brought forward over the crown of the hat. Small black safety pins can be used to gather any slack in the veil just under the brim at the back; extra hairpins into the bun can also help any minor fitting problems to achieve a smooth look. Veils can make a rider's complexion look slightly pallid, so careful use of make-up, including blusher and lipstick, should be experimented with beforehand.

Silk top hats are traditionally worn after noon at large shows and for final judging, especially if held in the evening. They are also worn for, and after, the opening meet out hunting. Bowler hats are correct at any other time, observing the neckwear rules.

A rigid **cane**, either leather covered or plain, is carried and should be no more than 1m in length (or 76cm for juniors riding ponies of 14.2hh and under).

Jewellery, other than tie pins, should be avoided. Earrings should be removed and any facial piercing, studs, etc. should not be worn.

TYING A VEIL

Elastic tied at X.

Veil pulled round face and over brim before tying the elastic loop to bring over crown of hat.

Elastic coming over crown and then smoothed into brim.

Veil in position with any slack or wrinkles smoothed out.

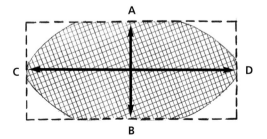

MAKING A VEIL
Measure from above brim of hat to under chin for A to B. Measure desired length (C to D) to go around hat (leave extra if you wish to tie the ends to secure them rather than use the elastic over crown method).
Round off the corners as shown and thread round hat elastic through the holes in the mesh all the way round.

CONCLUSION

Ladies have ridden side-saddle throughout the ages and it remains a graceful and elegant way to ride a horse. Many disabled riders find it an advantage to ride in this way, and ladies of advancing years have been able to continue their pleasure of riding into later life with the benefit of their side-saddles.

Advances in technology and fashions mean that modern living is ever changing and evolving, but side-saddle riding upholds the traditions and customs of a bygone era, which some consider to be romantic or simply fun. Whatever your reasons for choosing to ride side-saddle always remember to smile, enjoy your mount's company whether you own him or not, praise him whether or not you have done well together, thank him for trying to please you, and, finally, always value the time you spend with the horse.